Ambreen Razia

Ambreen is an actress and writer from South London. *The Diary of a Hounslow Girl* is Ambreen's debut show which premiered at Ovalhouse in 2015. Passionate about re-establishing British Asian comedy within the UK, she continues to write her comedy sketch show involving two British Asian girls exploring the clash between traditional Indian/Pakistani culture and modern British life.

She is also currently writing her next play *POT* primarily focusing on the recent comeback of 'gang culture within the UK.' Performance credits include: *On the Middle Day* (Old Vic Theatre); *Words and Women* (Edinburgh Fringe); *Random Acts* (Channel 4); *Fair Exchange* (Hen and Chickens Theatre); *Variations on a Theme* (Camden People's Theatre); *Mind the Gap* (National Theatre); *No Guts, No Heart, No Glory* (BBC 4 /Perth Festival Australia) and *Murdered by my Father* (BBC Three).

First published in the UK in 2016 by Aurora Metro Publications Ltd
67 Grove Avenue, Twickenham, TW1 4HX
www.aurorametro.com   info@aurorametro.com

The Diary of a Hounslow Girl © 2016 Ambreen Razia
Cover image © Talula Sheppard

With many thanks to: Ellen Cheshire, Simon Smith and Neil Gregory.

Printed in the UK by 4Edge Limited, Essex.
ISBN: 978-0-9536757-9-1

THE DIARY OF A
HOUNSLOW GIRL

by

Ambreen Razia

AURORA METRO BOOKS

THE DIARY OF A
HOUNSLOW GIRL

Tour Dates and Venues 2016

May 4 – 6	Ovalhouse, London
May 10	South Hill Park, Berkshire
May 12	Lighthouse Poole's Centre for the Arts
May 13 – 14	Theatre Royal Margate
May 17	The Drum, Birmingham
May 19 – 21	Stratford Circus Arts Centre, London
May 23	Antonin Artaud Theatre, Brunel University
May 24 – 25	Theatre Royal Bury St Edmunds
May 26	Bradford Literature Festival
May 28	Paul Robeson Theatre, Hounslow Arts Centre
June 1	Marine Theatre, Lyme Regis
June 3 – 4	Tobacco Factory Theatres, Bristol
June 7	The Brewhouse Theatre & Arts Centre
June 9	Upstairs at The Western, Leicester
June 10 – 11	Key Theatre, Peterborough
June 14 – 15	Queen's Hall Arts Centre, Hexham
June 16	Unity Theatre, Liverpool
June 17 – 18	Derby Theatre

The Diary of a Hounslow Girl is the third touring production from Black Theatre Live, a pioneering consortium of eight regional theatres. We are committed to effecting change for Black, Asian and Minority Ethnic touring theatre through a sustainable 3-year programme of national touring, structural support and audience development. Supported by Arts Council England, the Esmee Fairbairn Foundation and the Ernest Cook Trust.

It follows Black Theatre Live's previous successes in 2015 with *Macbeth* directed by Jatinder Verma and Pitch Lake Productions' *She Called Me Mother*, starring BAFTA award nominated actress Cathy Tyson.

The initiative is a partnership of Tara Arts (London), Derby Theatre, Queen's Hall Arts (Hexham), the Lighthouse (Poole), Theatre Royal Bury St. Edmunds, Theatre Royal Margate, Stratford Circus Arts Centre (London) and Key Theatre (Peterborough).

Our tours are supported by work with the Audience Agency, Mobius PR, Hardish Virk, King's College (London), Stage Text, Pilot Theatre and Outreach Associates at the consortium theatres.

In Autumn 2016 Black Theatre Live tours, in association with Watford Palace Theatre, *Hamlet* by William Shakespeare, directed by Jeffrey Kissoon, adapted by Mark Norfolk; the production will be a first in the UK with an all-black cast and director.

blacktheatrelive.co.uk | @BlackTLive

For Tara Arts on behalf of Black Theatre Live
Artistic Director: Jatinder Verma
Executive Director: Jonathan Kennedy
Associate Director: Claudia Mayer
General Manager: Alexandra Wyatt
Marketing Manager: Emma Martin
Technical & Operations Manager: Tom Kingdon
Development Officer: Francisco Ramos Zaldivar
Finance Manager: Xiao Hong (Sharon) Zhang
Capital Administrator: Martina Ferry
Black Theatre Live Tour Manager: Milan Govedarica

OVALHOUSE

Ovalhouse

Ovalhouse is a lively theatre and arts centre on the Kennington Oval, opposite the famous cricket ground. For the past 50 years, Ovalhouse has provided development and performance space to experimental, radical, and overlooked artists. Today Ovalhouse is known for theatre, performance and participation that speaks to a world beyond the mainstream. Ovalhouse is a leader in its field for organisations involved in creative participatory work with children and young people, and continues to be a vital home for boundary-pushing art, artists and audiences with an eye on the future.

In 2015 *Diary of A Hounslow Girl* was an original commission as part of 33% London, our highly acclaimed Creative Youth programme that builds on Ovalhouse's strong tradition of youth leadership. 33% London is creating a new audience of theatregoers while engaging with hard to reach communities through work with their artists; 33% is the percentage of Londoners under the age of 26.

ovalhouse.com | @Ovalhouse

For Ovalhouse
Director: Deborah Bestwick
Executive Producer: Stella Kanu
Director of Participation: Stella Barnes
Head of Youth Arts: Naomi Shoba
General Manager: Gary Johnson
Development Director Capital Campaign Katie Milton
Technical Manager Paul O'Shaughnessy
Head of Press and Marketing: Debra Jane Vannozzi
Press & Marketing Assistant: Emma Stirling
Finance Manager: Kwame Boateng
Finance Assistant: Kwame T B Antwi
Trusts & Foundations Manager: John Peterson
Fundraiser: Storm Patterson
Buildings Project Manager: Annika Brown
Participation Producer: Inclusion Cat Lee
Pastoral Care & Monitoring Officer: Katherine Mail
Development Coordinator Capital Campaign: Louise Cremin
Operations Manager: Alex Clarke

Supported using public funding by
LOTTERY FUNDED | ARTS COUNCIL ENGLAND

THE DIARY OF A HOUNSLOW GIRL

Written and Performed by Ambreen Razia

Directed by Sophie Moniram

Lighting Design by Paul O'Shaughnessy

Design by Petra Hjortsberg

Dramaturgy by Neil Grutchfield

Voicework by Rosa McRae

Project Management by Maeve O'Neill

Tour Stage Management by Amber Taylor

Produced by Black Theatre Live

Commissioned and supported by Ovalhouse

"Ambreen's writing is poetic in its structure and intensity, funny, moving, chilling, and delivered in a style that takes inspiration from spoken word and physical theatre. She has created a rhythm that draws the audience in, as compelling as a thriller, complete with gathering ominousness, shocks and comic relief."

– Deborah Bestwick, Director, Ovalhouse

"*The Diary of a Hounslow Girl* will be part of the opening season of the new £2.5 million Tara Theatre in 2016. The new theatre, with a dedicated rehearsal studio, will feature London's only indoor earth floor along with antique Indian doors, all encased within a tree motif on our façade, welcoming audiences and artists under its shade. Ambreen Razia's terrific play is exactly the kind of new work we wish to support in the new home of multi-cultural theatre in London. *Hounslow Girl* is a wonderfully funny take on a London phenomenon and one audiences will enjoy."

– Jatinder Verma, Artistic Director, Tara Arts

Biographies

Sophie Moniram – Director

Sophie trained on Mountview Academy's Theatre Directing MA. She directed the premiere of *The Diary of a Hounslow Girl* at Ovalhouse in 2015. She has also directed the premieres of *The Five Stages of Waiting* (Tristan Bates Theatre) and *F**king Outside the Box* (VAULT Festival). Further directing credits include *Creditors* by August Strindberg (The Cockpit Theatre), *Indian Summer* by Lucy Maurice (White Bear Theatre), *Purgatorio* by Ariel Dorfmann (Karamel Club) and *The Star-Spangled Girl* by Neil Simon (Karamel Club). She has developed new writing for VAULT Festival and Edinburgh Festival, and directed rehearsed readings at Soho Theatre and The National Theatre Studio. Assistant director credits include *The Rise and Shine of Comrade Fiasco* at The Gate Theatre (where she is a Creative Associate) and *Creditors* at The Young Vic. sophiemoniram.com

Paul O'Shaughnessy – Lighting Designer

Paul studied Stage Management and Technical Theatre Production in Vancouver, Canada. His Lighting Design credits include *Fat Man* (Ovalhouse and tour), *Singin' in the Rain* (London Oratory), *Autobahn* (King's Head Theatre), *Peter Pan* (Bloomsbury Theatre), *The Addams Family Musical* (Secombe Theatre) and *The Producers* (Arthur Cotterell Theatre). His Stage Management credits include *Oh! What A Lovely War* (Watermans Theatre), *Cake and Congo* (Theatre 503), *Our Town* (King's Head Theatre), *The Fastest Clock in the Universe* (Old Red Lion Theatre), *Merrily We Roll Along* (Watermans Theatre), *Saer Doliau* (Finborough Theatre), *Tu I Teraz* (Hampstead Theatre) and *The Clock / Radha is Looking Good* (The Pleasance). Paul is Technical Manager at Ovalhouse Theatre.

Petra Hjortsberg – Designer

Petra is an award-nominated theatre and performance designer who works internationally across Theatre, Dance, Opera and Film. She is Associate Laboratory Set Designer at Nuffield Theatre (Southampton) as well as Creative Associate at Gate Theatre (London). Recent theatre design credits includes *Juicy & Delicious* (Nuffield Theatre, Southampton), *Creditors* (Young Vic) *How To Win Against History* (Ovalhouse). Other Theatre Design credits includes the OFFIE Best Set Design nominated shows *Free Fall* (The Pleasance Theatre), *Occupied* (Theatre503), *Silent Planet* (Finborough Theatre), *Freak* (Theatre503, Assembly Rooms), *Companion Piece* (The Pleasance) and *Body Electric* (Best Production & Best Off-Site nominee, ABSOLUT Fringe Festival, Dublin). Associate Design credits includes *Moon Illusion* (Copenhagen Music Theatre) and *Land Of Our Fathers* (Trafalgar Studios, London and UK national tour). Film credits include: *Magpie, Way of the Monkey's Claw, The 95th, PubMonkey, Blind Man's Dream, For Better or Worse* and *Termination* (UK). In 2013, Petra exhibited at the international World Stage Design Exhibition. petrahjortsberg.com

Neil Grutchfield – Dramaturg

Neil has strong interest in and commitment to the development of new writing, developed through his career at the Royal Court Theatre, as New Writing Manager at Synergy Theatre Project, as Literary Manager at Hampstead Theatre and over 15 years as a dramaturg and script reader who has worked with first time, emerging, mid-career and senior playwrights. neilgrutchfield.com

Amber Taylor – Tour Stage Manager

Amber trained at Mountview as a postgraduate in Theatre Production Arts, specialising in Stage Management. She graduated from the University of Derby with a BA Theatre Arts in 2012. Recent credits include: As SM: *Tin Soldier* (The Arc Theatre, Stockton-On-Tees), *Pal Joey* (Karamel Club, London). As CSM: *She Called Me Mother* (UK Tour), *Inigo* (Pleasance Theatre, London) and *Berlin Cabaret* (Edinburgh Fringe, Derby Theatre Studio and Create Theatre Mansfield). As DSM: *13* (The Unicorn Theatre, London), *Angela's Ashes a Musical* (Derby Theatre & Lime Tree Theatre). As ASM: *A Level Playing Field* (Shoreditch Town Hall & University of East Anglia).

Rosa McRae – Voicework

Rosa trained in Voice at The Royal Central School of Speech & Drama before obtaining an MA in Theatre from The University of Leeds. She has taught Voice and Drama extensively across the adult and FHE sector as well as working for the V&A museum, The Tricycle and Clean Break Theatre. More recently, alongside her teaching Rosa founded and directed *Out of a Dream* which was an Arts in Health project, taking theatre, story and music into hospitals and health settings. The project was the recipient of an award from UnLtd – The Foundation for Social Entrepreneurs. Rosa is of dual English and Indian heritage.

Maeve O'Neill – Producer & Project Manager

Maeve is an independent arts producer, specialising in theatre producing and mentoring. Maeve has produced national tours for poet, Simon Mole, Novus Theatre, NIE Theatre and the first production of Blind Summit's award-winning show, *The Table* at Edinburgh 2011. She works on a freelance basis with artists, theatre companies and venues including Ovalhouse, Apples and Snakes and Jackson's Lane Theatre. She trained at The Gaiety School of Acting, Dublin and completed a BA in Modern Drama Studies at Brunel University. Current projects include *Work Play* by Nick Field and *Screwed* by Kathryn O'Reilly.

I was waiting with my best friend outside McDonalds after college when I heard her say...

'Look at her, Bruv'... Look at that
Hounslow Girl'.

Back in School I was surrounded by beautiful, confident, streetwise hijab-wearing Muslim teenagers who often led double lives. We would all stop at the chip shop after school and enjoy them on the way home, except one of my mates at the time who had to rush back home so she could get ready to go to the mosque.

Another had a boyfriend who wasn't Muslim, I swear I've never seen a girl whip off her hijab so quickly come three-thirty. We used to laugh about it. It was only when I got to college I realised that society had finally conjured up a name for these young women who try and balance their two co-existing worlds – 'Hounslow Girls'.

I dedicate this play to every girl in the world who is coming of age.

Ambreen Razia
2016

THE DIARY OF A HOUNSLOW GIRL

by

Ambreen Razia

The first performance was at Ovalhouse in 2015. This edition published to coincide with UK National Tour produced by Black Theatre Live with support from Ovalhouse.

CHARACTERS

SHAHEEDA – *The Hounslow Girl*

The play includes interjections from several additional characters which may be embodied by the same actor or others.

MUM

AISHA

TASH

LEONIE

AUNTIE NUSRUT

YOUTH WORKER

AARON

PHARMACIST

AARON'S MUM

Setting: Today

Part 1

The Opening

Music fades, lights go up on a small boxed bedroom.

A girl comes on stage with a patched up bruised nose dressed in a beautiful Salwar Kameez with a jacket on top; she is listening to music through her headphones. She puts her keys on the table and begins to hastily pack her things into a suitcase. She walks over to a video camera which is on top of her shelf; she sets it up and places it on her dressing table. She sits down and places herself directly in front of the camera, just as she is about to talk she receives a notification on her phone. She takes her phone out of her jacket pocket to have a look, she paces around her room nervously as she reads it. The notification has clearly disturbed her and through her unsettlement she addresses the audience.

SHAHEEDA Tash has been writing statuses all over Facebook saying she's gonna mash me up. *(She looks at the notification again.)* She keeps spelling words wrong which is making me feel a bit better and Leonie knows not to say too much in case I tell everyone about her and Mr. Coleman.

I mean it's not like I planned to stay friends with them forever. I know it's a bit of dickhead thing to say but Tash and Leonie don't ever plan to leave this place. Trust me, they're just not about that life. If I was to give Tash a *Vogue* magazine I guarantee you the first thing she would do is use it for roach and if I was to give Leonie the finest bottle of champagne she would shout out something like:

LEONIE Trust me, I've had willies bigger than this bottle. F.A.M!'

SHAHEEDA Anyway, my mum was bare happy when I stopped hanging around with Tash and Leonie because she says that it's better to be alone than in bad company, and her hope was that I would become best friends with Auntie Nusrut's daughter Yasmin, who's secretly just as bad but pretends to be so good.

Trust me just coz Yasmin can recite the whole Quran and speak fluent Urdu it doesn't make her an angel. I mean I've done some bad stuff but at least I don't pretend to be something I'm not, like I would never spark up a zoot before going into the mosque like she does! Or take my hijab off when I saw a group of boys. Yeah, I might have stolen a couple of things from Superdrug during the riots and dumb shit like that but at least I done it as myself.

You know when you do that thing when you're alone at school and you're pretending that your texting bare people? Really I was just going through my old pictures of me Tash and Leonie. I had a whole album from when we went down to Brighton together, them two just wanted to go cinema that day but

I thought it would be sick if we done something different, so we all packed up our shit and got the train down there and we sat by the sea all day sunbathing in our Primarny bikinis.

We must have posted a hundred Selfies that day; Leonie had her tongue out in most of them, showing off her new black and gold tongue-bar and Tash had just gotten her new nail extensions refilled so always had her two middle fingers up in every picture, hashtag no filter!

I remember asking Tash what she liked most about being by the sea, and half way through taking a toke of her spliff she said:

TASH   Pssh, I don't know... because it's free?

SHAHEEDA   And when I asked Leonie she said:

LEONIE   I don't know, babe. But if you think about it, thousands of people have lived without love but not one person has lived without water. Mad innit?

SHAHEEDA Leonie always surprised me with her views on the world, which is why I think I loved her the most. They both said to me that I wouldn't give a shit about the ocean as much if I wasn't in love, but they're wrong, I loved the sea before and I think it's because I've stood in front of so many things that make me feel small, but never free.

My sister chalked it up to the fact that I'm a Cancerian and I like the colour blue. *(She catches herself waffling on.)* Anyway, the point I was trying to make was that I didn't wanna go home that day. And our little trip to Brighton made me realize that there's more to life than Scatty Hounslow...

1.2

The Henna

She kicks off her shoes and begins to remove her jewellery. She begins stuffing things into a small duffel bag; throwing clothes aside she doesn't like then changing her mind.

SHAHEEDA   I need to hurry up and say what I need to say because I don't have much time. So usually there are nine parts to a Pakistani wedding – don't worry I'm not gonna go through all of them. My sister asked me if I thought she should go ahead and celebrate all nine. I was like, 'Aisha are you dumb?' The only thing you're doing is giving him nine chances to leave you, and I ain't trying to offend you or anything but trust me he doesn't love you that much. I wasn't being rude but if men have walked out on Jennifer Aniston and Marilyn Monroe then Walahi, the chances of him leaving her are proper high... especially if you're gonna give him nine chances.

So last week we kicked off with the henna.
(We hear faint sound of Indian music.)

Which is usually the first part to this
long event.

The bride ain't allowed to show her face
to no one on this day. Personally I think
it's in case someone recognizes her, if
you get me?

The only part of my sister I got to see
that day were her hands which would
slip out from under her veil, covered
in henna which had been prepared the
night before but you wouldn't think so,
it was already starting to fade and some
stupidsticious people say that the darker
the *mehndi* on the day of your wedding,
the longer you'll stay with your husband,
and hers was already turning into this
nasty burnt orange colour... swear down
she was so shook when she woke up
that day! And she was getting handed
these thick white and brown envelopes,
no one else clocked it, but she was giving
them all a slight shake to see who had
been most generous. I couldn't work
out where she was stashing them all;
I imagined she had sewn a kangaroo
type pouch on the inside of her knickers
or something. She was loving all the
attention, all the fuss that was being
made over her and her new man and
what pissed me off was that she done it
so well, like she got a Masters in being
a 'Top Pakistani Bride' and she would

do this thing where she would mimic those old 1920s Bollywood actresses by occasionally looking up and then giggle a bit and then look down. Pretending like she remembered everyone that was invited by saying: *(turns into her sister)*

SISTER   Thank you so much for coming Auntie, it's been too long.

SHAHEEDA   My mum was stood behind her chair not concentrating on anyone but me, holding her stomach every time she saw me checking my phone or moving closer and closer to the door.

1.3

First confession to Mum

The Music stops, the lights change. Back in the present.

SHAHEEDA   I just want her to let me tell the story and I can't have any interruptions from her, I mean I'm actually starting to scare myself with the thoughts I'm having, like you know, maybe tying her up and putting a bag over her head. *(She tries to look for a sympathetic face in the audience, someone who might support this idea.)* Nah... Joking. *(She walks over to the camera on her dressing-table, presses 'Record' and sits directly in front of it.)*

So just in case I ain't here when you get back, I won't miss out any important details and you won't be short-changed... this is fully it. The thing is... It's always been my dream to start fresh. *(Pause)* I wanna go travelling.

I want to visit the Far East first and I want to see The Great Wall of China, see what all the fuss is about. I want to meditate on top of a mountain and eat noodles with the locals and after I learn martial arts I wanna visit the Forbidden City coz I heard it's all off limits and that. Then I'd make my way down to South Africa and pay my respects to Mandela then move over to Egypt, see the pyramids, and for the final part of the trip, I'm gonna make my way over to America, drive down Route 66 and finish off at the Grand Canyon. You need to know that I'm different to everyone else around here, my dreams and aspirations go beyond anything anyone could ever imagine. I mean the only thing that I have in common with Hounslow is that I was born to leave it one day. *(She stops recording and goes back to the audience.)* You know when someone says one thing but they're always thinking another? That's her, that's my mum. She's about as fun as Andy Murray and when I ask my sister about why she's so complicated she says that all humans are complicated but as well as being complicated Mum's just spent her whole life trying to 'Look complicated', because she's been brought up to think that that's an attractive trait to have as a woman, and when she thinks we don't get all the suffering she's going through, she'll hit us with:

MUM   You will only realise when you become a mother.

1.4

An Unfair Start

She catches herself going off track again.

SHAHEEDA   Right back on track. I suppose I should start right from the beginning.

So I was the second daughter, which meant I had to be better than the first. High ambitions, lighter, slimmer and quieter... which I ain't. When my sister was born she had a full head of curly hair with big brown eyes and my mum's fat friend Auntie Nusrut glaring at her with her bright yellow teeth.

AUNTIE NUSRUT   This one will not let you down! The fair ones never let you down!

She had rosy cheeks with the longest lashes you had ever seen. Mum said she looked like a 'beautiful porcelain dolly'.

I was a strange looking baby. Mum said I looked like I'd seen a ghost when I was delivered, static hair, cross-eyed and a turned up nose. Auntie Nusrut glared over me too, not with big doughy eyes but with a look that probably made my mum wanna shove me back in.

AUNTIE NUSRUT Bismillah! Give her a bath with one gram of turmeric and half a glass of milk, tobah tobah, tobah... The dark ones always disappoint in the end.

SHAHEEDA Growing up, my sister would always try and get my eyebrows threaded, or stick blue contact lenses in my eyes. At my age, she was just normal, innit? She done everything properly. Mum says that even though I was the one wearing the hijab, I always the wild card, whatever that means. Sometimes I imagine I was swapped at the last minute! And my real mum was a wicked musician who couldn't afford to keep me because she had to rush off on tour. How sick would that be? My mum would always kill it! She'd never let me go to any parties. Oh my days! So a few months ago Shaun Ayres, one of the boys from our school was having a wicked house party, he'd hired out a DJ and everything! Kassem see this was the party of the year and just as I was about to leave my mum stopped me and said:

MUM *Tum kaha jariho?* Where do you think you're going in that bright top?

SHAHEEDA It's a Birds' and Bees' party Mum.

MUM Heh?!

SHAHEEDA   A Birds' and Bees' party! We have to go dressed as either a bird or a bee!

MUM   Why can't you wear your black and yellow shalwa kameez then? This party better not be in Brixton with all the blacks.

SHAHEEDA   I don't know Mum. I just accepted the event on Facebook innit.

MUM   You're on *Facebook?!* Your Auntie Nusrut told me that her niece went on *Facebook* – she met a boy and ran off with him! Now they're living in a council house in Hackbridge. One of those small one-bedroom flats with no double glazing and electric cookers. She has a baby on the way with an English boy. *Hai Hai! Tohoba Tohoba Tohoba Allah rem kareh! Uper jooah!* Go upstairs and put a shawl on please and take those wings off!

SHAHEEDA   You want me to take the wings off and put a shawl on? I'm gonna look homeless. And I've already posted a Selfie of myself on *Facebook* so people think I'm on my way.

MUM   *Tum Mussulman Hoh!* You're a Muslim girl. Remember, Shaheeda – you may be British, but you are not English.

SHAHEEDA   Mum, please let me go, everyone from school's going tonight, just allow it Mum, please!? *(Pause. Her face turns into a look of disappointment as if her mum has said 'No'.)* I spent ages doing my make-up that night, and I spent sixty pounds on those silver wings, and another twenty on that yellow top. My Mum doesn't get it! She grew up in Pakistan and didn't get invited to any parties. The closest she ever got to a party was her own wedding and even on that day she looked proper moody. *(Pause)* The earliest memory I have of my mum was seeing her crouched down on top of a prayer mat. She was muttering the words of some prayer... crying and trying to finish her Namaz with whatever breath she could find. It's like she was baring her soul to God and he was just straight up blanking her. Me and my sister were both watching through the crack in the door, too scared to go inside, and then she walked out and hugged us and said, 'It's just us now, it's just us girls.' That's why sometimes I don't listen when I go to my classes at the mosque, you know? Because half the time I don't think he's fucking listening, and if that's the case, then what's the point of fully practising?

My mum always says to me that by this age I should be able to cook at least one Indian dish. A lot of the time she compares me to our relatives' daughters who are able to juggle three chapattis on their heads while revising for their exams.

MUM   I hear Auntie Nusrut's daughter Yasmin knows how to make *three* Indian deserts. All from scratch.

SHAHEEDA   What she didn't know was that me and Yasmin would meet up every Wednesday after school and we'd blaze a little zoot behind the station, and she told me the only reason she learnt how to make those desserts was coz they're the best when you've got the munchies, innit? Rusmalai and Galab Jaman after a spliff! Oh my days. Mum said to me that if I still can't boil rice by the age of eighteen, she won't bother trying to find me a husband. 'No mother-in-law will have you,' she says. The day I mentioned Uncle Ben's microwavable rice her eyes filled with tears.

1.5

Second confession to Mum

She walks back over to the device and presses 'Record'.

SHAHEEDA   I can't stay here. I think I might die, or worse, I'll be alive but I'll be alive in Hounslow, and the thought of walking down Hounslow High Street one more time will definitely send me into some long-term depression. The sound of the shutters opening outside the same shops that sell the same things with the same people talking about the same shit... and actually walking back to the house I was thinking that it might be easier if me and Aisha both left you on the same day, then you can deal with the grief all at once, rather than spend your whole life wondering when I'm gonna leave you, coz I know you know it's coming, even though you don't know when. But to be fair, should I really have to worry about all that? You don't make any sense to me, coz you're the one who always says, nothing should hold us back, but actually it's you who's always in the way of everything. *(Stops recording, back to the audience.)*

I'm waffling. I'm wasting time which I haven't got, and I need to keep an eye on the time coz I reckon I got about thirty -five minutes before my mum and the rest come to the door and I don't know how many of them are coming, but if I set an alarm or something... *(She looks around her room goes over to her bedside clock and sets an alarm. She double checks it and places it back on her bedside table.)* Facts, stick to the facts! Facts are important, alright... Tash and Leonie: So Tash and Leonie became friends in Year 9. No wait! Year 10, but Tash moved to our school from a different school so didn't go to our school from the beginning, but me and Leonie became best friends in Year 11 but didn't chat before then so that's why them two were best friends so then... I can't do it like this. *(She takes a breath.)* Me and Leonie have always been best friends and I know Tash secretly hated that. Leonie is one of the buffest girls in school, and I ain't just saying that because she's my bestie, either! She's mixed race with long brown hair up to her bum, she looked like a video girl, better than a video girl! Leonie had these bright green eyes but you couldn't see them most of the time, usually because she was buzzing and had used a whole bottle of mascara on her lashes. *(She moves forwards towards the audience as though she doesn't want anyone to hear)* The thing about Leonie was that she was secretly seeing Mr. Coleman. He was our R.E teacher. Leonie said if any of us ever grassed her up or snaked her that Mr. Coleman would get done and that her older brother would kill him if he found out. Leonie never told us, but me and Tash knew her brother was part of some gang. His car was way too nice for someone who didn't work, and when Leonie would come to school with new Chanel earrings or a brand new Michael Kors watch, we just knew what time it was. *(Pause)* She loved Mr Coleman. And we loved her, which is why we never told anyone. Tash was mixed race too but not pretty, believe me when I tell you that Tash is a big girl. She was like our bouncer innit, always looked out for us. She had long, brown hair up to her bum too but everyone knew it was all weave, and had a sovereign ring on nearly every finger. Everyone knew Tash kinda fancied Leonie but no one would dare say anything. At school I was what you call a 'mid-level' student, not smart enough to make the school look good, but not dumb enough to be a success story either. At the beginning of Year 11 some Next woman came in to give us all a talk on 'Future careers and prospects' and she asked all of us what we wanted to be when we left school. Tash put her hand up and said a stripper, followed by Leonie, who said a coke dealer. The woman started sweating and rubbing the back of her neck then she fixed her eyes on me.

YOUTH WORKER What about you, young lady? What would you like to do when you leave school?'

SHAHEEDA Tash and Leonie started laughing at the blank expression on my face. I knew I had to come up with something quickly to avoid looking like some dickhead, so in the end I panicked and told her that I wanna be a terrorist. *(Pause)* I was expelled for a week and I was put in isolation for four days after I got back because I didn't write the letter of apology. That's when me, Tash and Leonie became close. I swear down, I had a whole album on my phone from all

the times we were in isolation together!
We'd spend the hours talking about
Leonie and Mr. Coleman. Tash would
usually be behind Leonie rolling her
eyes, thinking what we were all thinking.
We all knew what the deal was, but the
belief behind her bright green eyes was
mad scary sometimes. Like she actually
tricked herself into believing that he
took her to see *Cats* in the West End and
then they spent the evening drinking
'fine wines'. Fucking fine wines! *(Pause)*
If it wasn't for this trip, I would have
told everyone about Leonie and Mr.
Coleman. How he gave her a separate
phone that only he could contact her
on. Some old *Nokia* brick phone. How
he would pick her up from Hounslow
East and take her back to his house.
Fuck it. I'll tell everyone about when
he told her to get an abortion and how
she didn't leave her bedroom for three
days. Leaving her house and my white
top being covered in stains of mascara
from where she had been crying so hard.
I even took her to get it done. We sat in
that clinic filling out forms and reading
old *Heat* magazines for three hours
before we even got seen. *(She sits on the
edge of her bed, disturbed by the memory
she just recalled about Leonie. She looks
at the clock and quickly moves on to her
next point.)*

1.6

Mum's Memories

SHAHEEDA　　　I read somewhere that your memory is there to tie your past up with your present and provide a framework for your future, and it's our memories that make us who we are, and I just don't think I've got enough of the ones I want, to make me the person I wanna be. I mean me and my mum had some proper nice times together before all this happened. While my sister was at Uni we used to stay up and chat. She would tell me about her life in Pakistan and how free she felt when she was little, how she would sit outside in front of the open fire and watch my grandma work. Mum said my grandma would tell her about how she escaped from the partition, about the time they had to flee from their home because people were being massacred and that when she arrived at the station heavily pregnant, the train that came, after hers, was full of dead bodies. How her husband had left her and her unborn child and never came back. *(Pause)* My nan would always say that marriage is a gamble – a coin toss – and the day you get married is the day you flip it and pray that it lands on the right side. The day my mum got married and was about to leave for England, my grandma whispered something to her which she says she can't forget, even if she tried. Something like: "Remember your roots and remember what the English have done. Remember that you are British but will never be English." *(Pause)* Mum would tell me how Islam and her faith in Allah saved her from some scary situations. *(Pause)* On the first day my mum sent me to my classes at the mosque, she gave me a bag which was full of blue sugar paper and she told me to open it. Inside was a dark black hijab, she said that it was a veil that would protect me from all evil and maybe even save me from my own thoughts at times. It don't matter though, coz these memories are hers! Second-hand, which means I can't officially own them. I mean really, a memory is only a memory if you feel something when you think about it innit? *(Pause)* In Year 11, all the lessons meshed together: Miss Middleton's, Coleman's, Uncle Abdul Azeez's, my Mum's, Aisha's, and I ain't gonna lie, but those memories are way too shit for me to start building my future on. Up until a year ago, I never really felt a true connection to anything, not even a pair of trainers, and for me this was the beginning – the day I started all over again – the memories which would become the framework for my future. *(Beat)* The day I met Aaron. *(Beat)* Tash and Leonie used to call him a waste man because he didn't have a full-time job and he still lived with his mum, but I didn't care. I liked him from the second I saw him.

1.7

Aaron

Bus Stop. Lighting change to outdoors.

SHAHEEDA So there I was, fresh into year 11, standing at the bus stop with Tash and Leonie. We had our skirts rolled up and our new fresh *Air Maxes* on. They were both eating pick and mix, chatting about what a slag Tracy Brooker was. Tracy Brooker was some girl in our year that got pregnant by some next boy from a different school. Her Facebook and Instagram were covered in Selfies of herself, with her new baby bump on show at the bottom of every picture. She would post statuses like: "Me myself and I." Or: "The hardest battles are given to the strongest soldiers, ya get me!"*(Beat)* After she got pregnant, no one wanted to chat to her. Her mum had to take her out of school because people started making videos about her and posting them onto *YouTube*. Sometimes, we would see her around Hounslow, pushing her baby in the buggy with her head down, hoping no one would notice her.

Anyway! I definitely knew someone buff was coming over, coz Tash and Leonie started fixing their hair and pulling up their skirts as high as they could go and then I turned around and there he was. Leant on the 'Stop, Look, and Listen' poster, his face was only inches away from mine. I got really conscious of my breath so I pulled away. I sat down and crossed my legs which made my skirt ride up, revealing a little bit more of my thigh, and in his calm voice he said:

AARON   What you girls talking about?

SHAHEEDA   Tash and Leonie were still trying to recover, so I had to come up with something fast. "I was just telling Tash and Leonie about this new slimming diet I'm on." They both had tears in their eyes from laughing so hard. "You eat whatever you want before school then don't eat anything else all day, except chewing gum. You can eat chewing gum, not bubble gum like *Hubba bubba* or *Juicy Fruit* coz it's high in sugar but *Extra* and *Airwaves* is alright, and water! You can have water, but not tap water because of all the impurities and that, but *Evian, Buxton, Highland Spring...* mineral water! You can have mineral water. This mad thought ran through my head that if the 117 pulled up now I'd happily jump in front of it. He leant on the bus stop, looking at me in this strange, weird way, not in a way where he was tryin' a churpse me or anything but sort of like he felt a bit sorry for me, but kind of intrigued at the same time. *(Beat)* The moment was broken by Tash's big mouth. *(Turns into Tash)*

TASH   Say something then you fool...

SHAHEEDA   But I didn't have to. He took my phone out of my hand and started tapping away and then handed it back to me and said:

AARON   I'll call you later.

SHAHEEDA   I swear down, the High Street had never gone so silent. Leonie covered her mouth and Tash screwed up her face and everything froze. I was so proud of myself that day for not shouting out something dumb like WHEN?! I turned around to be hailed by Tash and Leonie, I imagined I'd soon wake up from this dream I was having and I'd be sat in my living room watching Auntie Nusrut chowing down the last shortbread but this was real... this was happening. Leonie looked deep into my phone like she wanted to climb into it.

LEONIE   Rahhh! Even his number's sexy, you know!

SHAHEEDA   Followed by Tash who said:

TASH   You need to check if it's legit and ring it.

SHAHEEDA   I knew it was legit. And I knew that I didn't have to ring anyone. My stomach was going mad that day and I had Justin Timberlake 'Take it from here' on repeat the whole time I was walking home. Apart from Justin, I don't really have any other man that I listen to. Except Uncle Abdul Azeez! One of the imams at the mosque, he's taught me since I was eight years old. He only teaches the girls. He says that girls need the most guidance and that they needed to embrace Allah on a different level, for only then we will be able to be fully obedient to the life which is laid before us. Sometimes I wouldn't listen because obedience wasn't one of the traits you needed, to be a traveller anyway. But occasionally he would say something which made me stop texting, something like: "Do not depend on Love, for it is rare, and do not depend on a human, for he is departing, rather depend on Allah for he is Supreme and he will never leave you." Shit. *(Back in the present, she grabs her phone and tries to ring the number again.)* Where the fuck are you? *(No one responds, she hangs up the phone.)* Where was I? *(Pause)* So the first time me and Aaron linked up, we went up to Leicester Square and I remember when we got up there it was proper busy and he didn't let go of my hand once. We got back to Hounslow East and it was proper cold so he gave me his jacket. It was too big for me but just to have it on, felt so nice. Now I know how Leonie feels when she links up with Mr. Coleman. Aaron would say the most beautiful things, so beautiful that even he had to sit back and reflect on what he had just said. When we got to the end of my road I remember he looked at me for ages and told me how pretty I looked that day and then he told me to close my eyes and open my hand. He had me standing there for ages – you never really knew how long Aaron's moments would last. He clutched onto my hand and I felt something in between our palms. He kissed the top of it and told me to open my eyes. *(Pause)* I'd never seen something so beautiful. He must have had to go into one of the Islamic shops to get it. It was a pink and blue hair pin for my hijab and it had diamonds in it. Uncle Abdul Azeez always said that 'The sun doesn't lose its beauty just because it's covered by the clouds and never should you'. It wasn't like buying a girl lip gloss to bring out her lips or mascara to bring out her eyes, but something deeper, like he was telling me to embrace my hijab and to wear it proudly. He stepped in closer to me and he lifted up my face and then finally he leant in for a kiss – my first ever kiss – and it was so much slower than I expected, plus his beard on the side of my face felt proper weird... now Leonie definitely underplayed it when she described her first kiss with Mr. Coleman, it was fucking mad! Madder and better than I ever imagined it to be. It was perfect. *(Pause)* So I had just started going out with Aaron and I swear down I would kill myself before I let him see me helping my mum carry the bulks of cardamom and basmati rice home, because we couldn't afford a car. This is my mum's ritual every Sunday before I had to go to the mosque.

MUM Why do you always walk with your head down? Stand up straight!

SHAHEEDA Mum, someone's going to see me! Allow it.

MUM *Mena Ye cube nay dekhe!* I have never seen anything like it. A girl who is so ashamed of her roots and her family.

SHAHEEDA I ain't ashamed.

MUM *Inshallah Shaheeda! Inshallah Allah Mia* will curse you with a daughter.

SHAHEEDA Alright, Mum!

MUM Then you will see how difficult it is, raising her in a country like this.

SHAHEEDA She was always chatting shit about something! I was following all the rules, I was learning Arabic like she wanted at the mosque and I only ever took off my hijab when I was in the shower, and even then she would look at me funny like it was supposed to be waterproof or something. I just wanted to get home that day, I left my mum at the front door and legged it upstairs. My phone was blinking – a *WhatsApp* message from Aaron asking me to come over.

I laid out three long-sleeved body-con dresses on the bed and four hours later I was ready.

Lighting change. A blue light. She is outside Aaron's front door and it's a cold evening.

SHAHEEDA   Seven o'clock. Before I had a chance to knock on the door, Aaron opened it and pulled me upstairs. I knew his mum was in because she was up, singing along to *Strictly*. He closed his bedroom door and locked it. His room was foggy and smelt of weed and antiseptic. Aaron's back was covered in roots. Roots of the Kapok Tree, for those of you who don't know – it's one of the only trees where the roots spread out and grow on the surface as well as underneath, so you can see all its imperfections in its growing process, and even though the roots wanna travel in every direction it's still proper grounded into the earth. And when he would take his top off, the whole tree began to move and the roots would spread down his back and the thorns which travelled around his waist led up to the stems on his arms which were both covered in full sleeves of dark red roses and just above his forearm was a woman's eyes filled with tears along with a pocket watch on the other. I had never seen such a beautiful canvas, it was better than all the Wonders of the World which I had only ever seen in my travel books. Aaron's a tattoo artist. He said school wasted his time which is why he left and would always say that truly creative people can't follow the education system anyway. *(Beat)* He had this globe in his room, and he would land the tip of his finger on all the places that he had been to and then tell me about all the different cultures he'd experienced while he was there, and how he'd always come back a better artist. I would love watching him move around his room, the way he would touch things so delicately like everything had a pulse, the way he would move over to his plant and pick the best buds for us to smoke and the way he would lick the edge of his *Rizla* and always give me the first pull. Getting high with Aaron was different. I mean Tash would always have one pre-rolled when we got to hers so we never really knew what was in it and whatever it was, it just used to make us chat shit, but Aaron would talk about that deep shit! Like vibrations and energies that we're surrounded by, and how important it was for us to just live in the moment. He would then stop half-way through his sentence and tell me how much he loved my eyes and my skin. He sat on the edge of his chair and he put both his hands around my face and asked me if I noticed anything different.

AARON   Look closer, Shaheeda, he said.

SHAHEEDA   And then I saw it. I had to look at it for about ten seconds before I believed that my name, Shaheeda, was written across his chest. It was only small but underneath it was the Arabic translation. I read somewhere that when the air temperature around you is above 99 degrees Fahrenheit, you need to sweat just to control your body temperature and at that moment Aaron's room got proper hot. *Kassem se,* there was something so exciting about it, though I kinda liked it, everything about it, even the font he used! Bold, edgy which he said represented my spirit and the Arabic translation made the whole thing feel holy – ritualized, you get me? And then he presented me with one of his moments – the moment which changed everything. He raised his eyebrows and said:

AARON   Will you come away with me? *(She freezes.)*

SHAHEEDA   I think I must have been frozen for at least ten seconds before I said – Are you dumb? *(She can't contain her excitement and is overwhelmed by complete joy.)* Yes! Yes! I'll come. Before I had a chance to think I could smell the antiseptic again and I felt the tracing paper hit my lower back, then the feel of his rubber gloves as they gripped my hips and held me still which made my heart race but my body was static. I could feel him wiping off the beads of sweat which had started to form on my back from where I was so nervous. After it was over, I lied on his chest, listening to his slow steady heartbeat which was so different to the speed of mine and I could hear my sister's voice in my head telling me that it was *haram* to have a tattoo and that if I got it, I wouldn't be able to have a proper burial, but it was something that would always tie us together, so when Aaron would go travelling or not call me for days at a time, it didn't matter because he would always bring the world back with him. He would tell me about the Seven Wonders of the World and how I would feel when I was stood in front of each of them, whilst he drew around the outline of my tattoo with the tip of his finger – his name which he wrote so well, it made me feel connected to him in ways that henna couldn't. *(Beat)* He took me down to Oxford for the day and we stopped at a spot which overlooked one of the University buildings – The Chapel of Keble College – which was proper old and ancient. He held me close and kissed my lips and slipped something into my pocket... and there it was, the concrete to his promise, the last brick to his pyramid, and the root of his word – a round-the-world ticket.

And at that moment Hounslow didn't exist. It was wiped off the planet and there was nothing left of it.

He put his hands on my waist and said:

AARON   "O ye women, wrap close your cloak,
So you won't be bothered by ignorant folk,
You can climb mountains or cross the seas,
Expand your mind in all degrees,

With the right to prosper and the right to grow
Whether it be fast, steady or slow
The feelings you have now
Won't disappear overnight,
But somehow, someway...
everything will be alright."

SHAHEEDA   Miss Middleton taught us poetry for a whole year, but I never fell in love with it till that day. I went home and recited the poem to my sister, Aisha, but she just crossed her arms, leant back on the kitchen counter and said:

AISHA   Wake up, Shaheeda.

SHAHEEDA   My mum was finding it hard to look at me. I'd covered all my tracks but she sensed something was going on. Aaron said that everyone gives off energies... Maybe she could see mine? Maybe she could see the places that I was going reflecting off me and maybe she couldn't stand it because she was stuck here, but as much as I felt ready to be stood in front of the Seven Wonders, I still felt like some dickhead stood in front of her. *(She has a sudden thought.)*

What if she finds out and she marries me off? What if I'm like shipped off to Pakistan secretly and they'll drop me to the airport and do some MI5 shit where they tell me to put my phone in a scary brown envelope and then replace it with like a *Nokia* 6210. Then they delete *Facebook*, my *Insta*, and my *Snapchat!*

Change my passport, wipe me off the face off the planet and get me married off. To some fat, lazy, forty year-old man who lives in a remote village in Pakistan somewhere, and we won't have a TV, and if we did I wouldn't be allowed to watch it anyway, because I'd be outside looking after his goat in the back garden, which is obviously named after some famous Pakistani cricketer coz he thinks that's bare cool. *(Beat)* And then Aisha's voice rang through me one more time.

AISHA   Wake up, Shaheeda.

SHAHEEDA   And I did. I woke up and realized that I had officially missed two of my core exams – Maths and Science, which meant I was gonna fail anyway and I had ignored my mum's calls all day and that I was supposed to go to Leonie's house and cover for her while she was out with Mr. Coleman. I fucked up but there's no room for it in my future. I knew that there were loose ends that I had to tie up but it was too late. Tash was already looking to mash me up and Leonie weren't gonna stop her so confronting them didn't quite go the way I had planned...

1.8

The Fight

SHAHEEDA Last week I was on the 117 after leaving Aaron's and both Tash and Leonie jumped on with Miss Dynamite blaring from Tash's phone.

Scene changes to a night bus. She moves as though the bus is moving.

SHAHEEDA They were sat on the two middle seats at the back of the bus with their brand new leopard print *Air Maxes* on and doughnuts in their hair that were the size of their heads. I heard them whispering from the back

LEONIE Do you think she's ever gonna come back to school?

TASH Nah coz, she's got too comfortable now innit?

SHAHEEDA You see, what they didn't realize was that they were going to be here forever. They'll be catching this same bus in ten years' time! Signing on! Going back and forth to the Job Centre on Lampton Road with their babies crying and screaming in the push chair. Stuck in Hounslow for good. I calmed myself down and sunk deep into my thoughts. I started thinking about Route 66 and me and Aaron parked on the edge of the Grand Canyon, him holding me by the waist and gazing into my eyes.

TASH   OI!

SHAHEEDA   I was less annoyed at Tash for shouting at me and more annoyed that she disturbed my thoughts of Aaron. I held my tongue and looked ahead.

TASH   Did you not fucking hear me!?

SHAHEEDA   I could feel the palms of my hands getting sweaty and the handles of the bag slowly disappearing into my clenched fists. My whole body felt like it was on fire and my hand tightened round the pole. I could hear Leonie's squeaky giggle while Tash was kissing her teeth, staring me out. I could see Leonie getting awkward so she turned towards the bus window and started drawing pictures of dicks and spliffs, anything that she hoped could get Tash's attention, but Tash opened her big mouth and turned everything upside down

TASH   You're just a fucking Hounslow Girl, Shaz. And you're one dumb bitch if you think you're getting out of here.

SHAHEEDA   I looked down at my *Air Maxes* and the *Nike* ticks were all fuzzy. Miss Dynamite's voice started getting louder and louder and the sound of the bus doors opening was piercing through me. I started breathing faster and heavier then I let go of the pole and grabbed Leonie by the hair and I was screaming in her face like I was possessed. I can't be sure but I think I punched her like four times and I was meant to go for Tash but Leonie was in the way and then I thought Tash was going to rush me once I jumped Leonie but she just started crying. I must have looked like a psycho to make Tash cry, I mean she was rushed by a group of boys once and didn't even cry then. I got off at the backdoors and I could see Tash mouthing the word 'Sket' from the bus window. I fixed my hijab and just chalked it up to pure jealousy.

1.9

Shaheeda's 'Mystery'

SHAHEEDA   Imagine, right... some people will die without ever having had a chance to experience true love. Take my sister, she don't know what true love is! What? Just because everyone in the community celebrated her marriage? It doesn't make her love any deeper than mine. No one round here could ever understand how deep our love was, it was only something that could be felt and only between the two of us, Yeah! I know Tariq's taking my sister on her 'fancy' honeymoon but Aaron didn't have to marry me to open up the world to me, he said that if you loved someone that much you would do that for them regardless.

Walking home from the bus stop I could feel the streets of Hounslow turning into sand underneath my feet, the sound of the shutters closing and becoming the busy market stalls of the Far East, I felt like if I was to go home and touch my bedroom walls they would crumble into dust because nothing mattered anymore, nothing was real, and when nothing feels real, it becomes easy to lie.

About a month ago Aaron asked me to stay at his house for the first time in a whole year. He said it's gonna be a special night so I spent a good hour coming up with something to tell my mum: 'Mum, I know it's last minute but I was wondering if I could stay over at Yasmin's House?'

This was the first time I had said anything to her in a month. She's not been the same with me since Oxford, she keeps holding her stomach when she sees me, probably thinking about what the worst-case scenario could be and how she'll have to cope with the shame of whatever it is. *(She takes a deep breath. Lighting change, Outside Aaron's front door)*

Seven o'clock. Before I had a chance to knock on the door, Aaron opened it and pulled me inside. *(She enters Aaron's room.)* The smell of weed and antiseptic was stronger than ever. He sat crouched over his bed, using his folder full of sketches to roll up on. I inhaled his smoke and put my hand on his chest, covering up some of the letters of my name. He looked at me with that deep stare and if I wasn't so in love with him I would have told him to stop making moments out of everything! I could feel my heart beating, faster, something I was used to by now. He kissed me on the lips and said:

AARON   Don't you think it's about time you showed me your hair? *(She looks surprised.)*

SHAHEEDA   I told him it weren't even all that and then he kissed the top of my head and he told me that nothing in this world was worth being scared of, especially not him... I told him that it wasn't just my hijab, it was part of my mystery, and what separated me from the rest. Uncle Abdul Azeez said that women who wear the hijab are like pearls in a shell, protected, and without it we would get washed up by the ocean, which is full of sharks which wanna hurt us but I knew Aaron wasn't that. He loved me, he looked at every part of my face and then slowly unpinned the pink and blue diamond hair pin, which held everything together so beautifully, and then he said:

'She chose to hide,

Behind her veil.

In her safe home,

Her existence frail.

Her identity and her honour,

Her own choice to preserve.

Hiding within her soul,

The Modesty she reserves.'

(She begins to unwrap her headscarf on stage as she recites the poem.)

'Proud of her identity,

Happy in her choice.

This is what she is,

Her cloth no longer her voice.'

(She reveals her hair to the audience for the first time.)

When I woke up, Aaron wasn't there, and for the first time I had seen his room in light, not daylight, or twilight, or even sunlight, nothing mystical or magical like that, but it was just this grey concrete gloomy colour which washed over the room – Hounslow light. His tattoo templates that covered his floor were gone... The ones I used to have to tip-toe or hop between to get to him, and the poetry which used to line the walls was gone. There was no order to anything, nothing had a set place and this wasn't how it was supposed to feel. I crept out of his house in the early hours of the morning, and Hounslow High Street felt a little bit like that scene from *28 Days Later*, no one in sight but I could feel my mum's presence as I walked home. You see my mum already had a solid plan in her head of where we were gonna end up and without ever telling us she expected us to figure it out. That ain't fair, is it? There was no time for mistakes, no room to step off her pre-planned path and do a gram of MDMA in a park somewhere, or get caught shoplifting! That never stopped me before but this was different. What's the word Mr. Coleman used to describe Mary Magdalene? Tarnished, something sketty like that. Uncle Abdul Azeez says that none of us are angels, but he said as long as you catch yourself in moments of temptation and immediately turn back to Allah then Inshallah, he'll allow you back in his good books, which sort of meant we could just do whatever we wanted, and kinda get away with it.

Part 2.1

The Registry

SHAHEEDA	It was the day of the registry, the second part of this mind-numbing wedding; the paperwork, the bit your Uncles and Cousins can't be bothered to sit through, and why should they? No free parking, No free food and no gossip. My mum was running around trying to find my sister's earrings and I could hear her shouting at me from downstairs telling me to get out of bed and help her look for them but I was just staring deep into my phone and waiting for it to ring. My morning ritual, waiting for Aaron to tell me he couldn't get any signal where he was, which is why he hadn't rung me in six weeks.
MUM	*Neechay aana!* Come downstairs!
SHAHEEDA	They're probably on top of the microwave, just wait innit!
MUM	*Neechay aana! Ek larka darwaazaa par he!* There's boy at the door!
SHAHEEDA	YES! I was relieved that he'd finally come to his senses and decided to stop ignoring me. Come to pick me up, maybe? Whisk me off earlier than planned, whatever his reasons were for blanking me, I could never be angry with him. I just needed to see him. My mum was at the bottom of the stairs, she

had her hands on her stomach again, preparing herself for what was about to happen... The moment she had been waiting for these past few months and then my stomach sunk when I got to the last step. She looked right through me and said:

MUM   Shaheeda. Inshallah. Allah will forgive you. *(Pause)*

SHAHEEDA I couldn't take my eyes off her, they followed her to the doorway of the living room, she looked back at me without saying a word and slammed the door. Those words rang through my head and I tried to think of all the different ways I could seek forgiveness while still having what I wanted. I couldn't help but think Allah was testing me and he was presenting me with two doors. I just wanted him to be straight with me and tell me whether I should put my mum out of her misery, open the living room door and tell her everything, or was this the part where I chose love? I walked over to the front door shaking with fear and excitement and then... *(She reaches the door. She stamps her foot on the floor and throws her head back as though she has been punched in the face. There is blood all over her nose, she sits down on the edge of her bed and recovers. She holds her nose back and starts to wipe it clean. She paces around her room while trying* *to wipe her nose working herself up into a state. She aggressively starts to go through her duffel bag and eventually throws her duffel bag across the room. She gathers herself and begins to shove everything into her suitcase; she zips it up and continues.)* Leonie's brother found out about what happened on the 117. My nose was full of blood, leaking all over the carpet and before anyone had a chance to see, I left the house and forgot my hijab, my mystery was at about a zero and I didn't even know where I was going! But my nose was fucked! Probably broken and I had to get it sorted before the registry so I stumbled into *Boots* on Hounslow High Street for the pharmacist to look at and I thought while I was there and unrecognizable I'd deal with the other thing I was putting off but I couldn't bring myself to put it on the counter, so instead I started picking up anything and everything I could find, chewing gum, *Tic Tacs,* Eyeliner, the leaflets which didn't cost anything followed by the pregnancy test I had in my hand... covered in sweat. The pharmacist looked at me and up and down and spoke louder than he needed to.

PHARMACIST Can I help you?

SHAHEEDA Just what I needed... Some six foot glorified Indian pharmacist who didn't make it as a doctor, looking at me up and down with a look on his face that said 'What a waste.' I leaned over the counter and said: 'I need a bandage for my nose.'

PHARMACIST Which kind do you want?

SHAHEEDA Which kind have you got?

PHARMACIST Well, there are different bandages for different reasons. This one, for example, is for temporary injuries and needs to be changed once a day and this one is for more permanent damages, mainly used if the harm that's been caused is irreparable or needs major medical attention.

SHAHEEDA I couldn't work out why this dickhead was shouting at me like I was at the other side of the shop. 'I'll take the second one. Please.'

PHARMACIST Of course you will. Can I help you with anything else?

SHAHEEDA He kept looking at me with this long stare probably thinking that if I was his daughter he would wash his hands of me immediately. The mixture of the pain and the anger that was built up made me lose all sense of myself. 'Look man! I've missed my period alright! So just give me three more tests, so I can go home. Oh and by the way, the Prophet, he don't allow contraception, if it's done for vain or for selfish reasons alright!'

She steps out of the action and is back in the room.

SHAHEEDA   I'll tell you this for nothing, but this idea that everyone has in their head that a Muslim Bride is pure and innocent till her wedding night is pure gas. That her husband's going to take her to some fancy hotel on a beach and they're gonna experience each other's bodies for the first time is the biggest lie you will ever hear. My sister had loads of boyfriends before Tariq, you know? White Black, Chinese, Indian, Middle Eastern, Italian, Caribbean, Bulgarian, Romanian, Lithuanian, French. Believe me when I tell you that Aisha has tasted every cuisine before her main course. So her mystery is fake. *(Beat)* I just knew I had to get through this wedding and then I'd be out of here. *(She takes a deep breath.)*

So there we were at the registry watching this boring shit. I spent most of the day in the toilet, trying to cover up my broken nose with lumps of concealer, hoping no one would notice and I just kept hearing echoes of my mum's voice throughout the day, telling people that I fell down the stairs. Hounslow couldn't have felt closer and it was suffocating me with everything that it had.

I don't know whether it was because I was high on Tash's paracetamol but the guests looked more and more cartoon-like as the day went on, their teeth were bigger, their laughs were louder and

I tried to ring Leonie, from the toilet cubicle, but it kept going through to voicemail. I wanted to tell her that I didn't mean what happened on the bus.

While Aisha and Tariq's vows for each other were getting sanctified in the name of Islam, I kept opening my clutch bag and looking at my ticket which was neatly sat next to my lip gloss, I needed to be certain about something, anything! So I ran my fingers over to the gate number, which I had memorised so well, then across to the seat number trying to work out who out of the two of us would be sat next to the window, but I couldn't because I didn't know where Aaron was sat, whether we were sat together or whether he had just booked whatever seats were free and as hard as I looked I could only see my seat number so I looked at the email confirmation on my phone which he had sent me to see if there were any more clues on that but there was nothing... Nothing that showed a booking for two people, one departure time, one seat number and one ticket.

She stops and freezes as though she realizes something, she gets up and begins shaking her head in disbelief, she begins muttering to herself.

One Ticket.

She sits in disbelief.

I had this fucked up dream the night before that I got out the shower and my tattoo was gone, and everything I touched crumbled, but it didn't turn into the sand that I had so often imagined, but dust. Leonie ain't been the same since she came out of that clinic, you know? I can't explain it, but now it takes a little bit longer for her to get our jokes, and sometimes she would just be in her own world, I would usually give her a big hug or trip her up, anything to snap her out of that daze. *(Pause)* We got home that night and Aisha kicked off her heels. Mum got comfortable in the living room and the house was finally still. I crept past Aisha's room towards the bathroom. After lining up the fourth test on the glass shelf everything started spinning. It was a clear win for the crosses, a positive verdict and all I could hear was the sound of bangles hitting the sink as I tried to get my balance back and everything began crumbling until I was met by a sound which scared me more than anything, more than what I had just discovered. Mum crying. *(Beat)*

I wanted to go into that living room and instead of hugging her and comforting her, I wanted to fucking shake her and say, "Mum do you know what I needed from you, do you? I needed you to tell me about the day you fell in love and how you coped when you had your heart broken, the first time you were caught sneaking out the house to meet a boy or your first kiss, instead of always trying to distract us with Arabic lessons and lectures, spending your whole life tryin' a make us learn a language and a religion which we can't ever truly understand while living in this city – your version of what you thought could truly save us when really it was so much more simple than that: a touch, a hug, a brief conversation." I read somewhere that it only takes a few weeks before a baby can tell the difference between its mum and other adults, and the voice and smell of the mother can be recognized from birth, so that means you're pretty much fucked from the very beginning.

She gathers herself ready for the final event.

Part 3.1

The Valima

SHAHEEDA Finally we had the Valima, which is where I've just come back from. It was held at the Islamic Integration Community Centre on Staines Road. I went round the corner and tried to call Aaron who still wasn't answering his phone, followed by Leonie who was straight up blanking me... that apocalyptic feeling was well and truly back, I moved towards the entrance and I was stopped by Uncle Abdul Azeez, he looked at me and asked me how I was. *(Surprised at his calm response.)* I don't know why I did it, but I actually told Uncle Abdul Azeez I was going to have a baby. Out of all people, mad innit? I stood at a distance though! Ready to fly kick him in case he tried to grab hold of me and drag me inside but he didn't, he stood up straight and clasped his hands in front him. He took a breath and said that everything has already been written for us, everything is *Makhtub*. He said my child *Makhtub* indicates that Allah has written everything already and that people should not fear because we are all in good hands. He said that it is Allah who writes our destinies but I couldn't help but think that Aaron had a part in writing mine. He put his hand on my arm and told me that God understands everything, then he just sort of gracefully glided off... *(Pause)* The celebrations were still going on inside and my sister and Tariq looked proper loved up. The waiter brought round Shrimp starter's from Iceland's 'Taste of the Orient' section, but my mum said I wasn't allowed to tell anybody that.

MUM *(Quietly)* *Kuch nay Kehna!* Don't speak unless you can improve the silence. *Teekeh!*

SHAHEEDA   The Valima is where the couple have their first dance and they bring out the ten-storey cake. This is where most of the pictures are taken, and when developed looks a bit like a second-hand rainbow and just as semi-detached as the houses round here.

Oh my days, the aunties were all barling, some of them even fell to the floor! As soon as I went to go and help one auntie up another one had thrown herself down across the room and by the third drop, I just let them all pile up, innit. *(Beat)* I was watching my sister and Tariq have their first dance and I was thinking about all these different things – like how will I know if it's left-handed or right-handed? Or what if it's allergic to something and I don't know until it's too late? Or what if fat Auntie Nusrut stands over me and tells me there's something wrong with it. I could see my mum looking at me like she wanted to come over, but she didn't. My hands got sweaty and I began to burn up. I was thinking about the walls crumbling in my dream and the thought of travelling the world on my own scared me more than anything! One fucking ticket? I couldn't help but think that this was one of his moments again! One of his stupid, epic, free-spirited grand gestures. Was he trying to teach me something about being independent, because I didn't want that! I wanted stability, like the roots of the Kapok tree. I didn't want a teacher or a philosopher, I wanted to be loved! I looked up and I was starting to see double — double the guests double the decorations, and worst of all double the huge luminous green cake that Tariq's mum had ordered which looked like it had come straight out of a nuclear power plant, and I felt myself being drawn towards it, like it was the only thing that was gonna be able to hold my balance if I was to fall... *(Beat)* My mum's eyes widened as I got closer and closer towards it, and out of nowhere I was tapped on the shoulder by Fat Auntie Nusrut and as I swung around my arm whacked straight into the fifth tier of the cake which frisbeed straight on to my sister's lap, painting her gold dress with nuclear green cake which now made her look like the inside of an avocado! But that wasn't all coz the cake didn't slow my arm down which was only stopped when my fist connected with Auntie Nusrut's fat face. While Tariq's mum was desperately trying to stop the rest of the cake from toppling over I found myself saying how sorry I was and that I would clean it up but the more and more I started to clean it up, I felt sick. I caught a glimpse of my sister with her hands over her face and I don't really remember how this happened but I managed to find my way on to the middle of the dance floor, and everyone was looking at me. My mum was standing in the corner of the room paralysed and I felt this horrible feeling, something rising up from the pit of my stomach, all the way up through my chest and into my throat and as I went to turn around to tell everyone not to worry, my sister got in the way and I vomited all over her green and gold nuclear dress. *(She stands still and holds the stage in an awkward silence.)*

No one moved. If anything was gonna be the death of my mum, it was this very moment. I was having a bit of an outer body experience when I felt Tash's paracetamol kick in which made me start slurring, 'It's okay, I'll fix it, I'll fix it, just fucking calm down everyone, yeah.' *(Pause)* The aunties and uncles were gasping, and I was stumbling around in search of something to mop it up with, but the closest thing to me was my sister's scarf which I so shamefully pulled off from around her neck and started wiping up the vomit, and as I was on the floor she calmly lifted my head up and said:

AISHA   What is it, Shaz?

SHAHEEDA   I looked at her, ready to tell her everything, about how I fell in love and lost my two best friends, didn't do my GCSEs, discovered things about myself that I never really knew, like my love for poetry, and that I'm gonna be a mum... at sixteen, and that I wished I could have been like you and could have done everything by the book but there's something either very wrong or very right with me and I can't work it out because I haven't had time because... Because... *(She pauses, catches her breath and exhales.)* And before I had a chance to speak I felt my mum grab me by the arm and say:

MUM   *Kya hogya tomhe? Abka shakel itna harab he!* If you can't be happy Shaheeda, then go home.

SHAHEEDA   I wasn't going to cry. Not in front of all these people and just as I felt my chest tightening and the tears coming, I legged it. I left the Valima, I ran through Beaverfield Park, down Heathdale Avenue, and I could see the Integration Centre getting further and further away as I looked back, disappearing into the distance and people were looking at me like I was fucking crazy, running through Hounslow with my salwar kameez, like I was running away from my own wedding or something. *(Beat)* I ran so fast that I got to Aaron's house in the space of ten minutes. I wasn't even sure about what I was there to say, or what he was gonna say when he saw me in the state I was in. I rung his doorbell and there was no answer but his window was wide open and he always closed it when he went out so I thought he must just be blanking me like he had been doing for the past six weeks when I needed him the most and I couldn't work out why, I mean I didn't know what I had done to mess this all up? Fuck it. Aaron?

Lights dim. She is looking up at a window.

SHAHEEDA   I've tried to ring you, but your phone's off. I just wanted to let you know that I'm ready. Packed! And I know you've seen all my messages this month coz I can see the double blue ticks on all the *WhatsApps* I've sent. *(She looks around her as if she is standing outside his window and people are walking past.)*

Look. This thing I need to chat to you about, it's important. Like proper important. Like World War Three important ... *(Pause, she waits for a response.)*

I saw Miss Middleton at Hounslow East, she stopped me and said that I'll have to retake my GCSEs next year with Sinead O'Brian and Lacy Adams. She said that I had a lot of potential, you know? Her exact words were that I have 'a natural ability to retain information and I just get things quicker and that if I had put it to good use I'd be a proper success.' And do you know what I said? Aaron, do you know what I said?

I said that I remember what Aaron was wearing when I first saw him. I could tell you every single tattoo he has and what they all mean. I remember our first kiss like it was yesterday and how both his eyebrows rise when he's waiting for an answer to a question. I told her not to worry and that my ability to retain important information had been put to good use. *(Pause)* Aaron? And then I heard her, for the first time in a whole year, I finally saw her. She was nothing what I expected, bigger than I had imagined, wearing a little leather skirt that was too tight for her, and her reading glasses which pushed her hair back, she looked at me and said:

AARON'S MUM Can I help you?

SHAHEEDA Yeah, I'm looking for Aaron. She looked at me up and down, like she had never seen such a walking, talking colourful mess like this in her life, maybe because I was covered in vomit and my mascara had smudged across my face and I had a patched-up nose and I think I might have actually scared her a bit, and then she said:

AARON'S MUM He's gone, love. *(Pause)*

SHAHEEDA Do you know when he'll be back? She looked at me like she wanted to give me a hug. I know she did! But I don't think she knew where to start.

AARON'S MUM I don't know. Tomorrow? Six weeks, six months, I really can't tell you. He does this.

SHAHEEDA I wanted to ask her ten thousand questions. Did he tell you where he was going? Did he ever mention me? Do you know who I am? But I didn't. No words were exchanged but we shared something in common, both victims of his departure, and I realised that I wasn't the only one who he had left behind, and even though she looked emotionally intact, and happier than my mum on the best of days, there was some kind of grief that sat with her, and I think I might have just rocked up and reminded her of something that she was desperately trying to ignore. I thought about something that Uncle Abdul Azeez said, that Allah talks about the duty towards your mother three times in the Quran and in Islam it's written that paradise is beneath your mother's feet, and the love of a mother is unparalleled to any other and that as children we have responsibilities to honour that... but I also couldn't help think that Heathrow Airport was only a train ride away, freedom was that close. I could come back once the dust had settled. I could *WhatsApp* my mum then pick up my suitcase and take flight. Then half way through my day-dreaming, I could see her still standing there... looking at me, leant against the door frame like she had seen that whole little dream sequence just run through my head and I thought, how many other hopeful dream sequences had she seen in her time? Then she smiled at me and she looked just like Aaron and before she went inside and was about to close the front door which I had been stood in front of more times than she'll probably ever know she said:

AARON'S MUM Go home. *(Pause)*

SHAHEEDA Back I went through Beaverfield, down Heathdale Avenue, people still looking at me like I was crazy which I probably am, crazy that I chose to walk down Hounslow High Street one more time before setting myself free from this place, crazy that instead of wanting to see the depth of the Grand Canyon, I was more worried about how my mum was feeling right now... How nothing could get worse and nothing made sense but one thing was for sure, that there was no longer sand beneath my feet walking down Hounslow High Street... and that I sort of didn't mind the concrete pavements any more. *(Pause)*

When I got home just now, the house felt different, and as I walked past the family pictures hung on the landing, I noticed that the only one that wasn't framed was my mum's wedding photo, maybe she didn't think it was worth framing but wanted to make sure me and my sister understood that we did come from something special – we were born out of love even if it fell apart somewhere down the line, and it's mad that she didn't know what was ahead of her back then, that the man who she called her husband would leave her with a baby all by herself in a country she wasn't familiar with – just like my grandad did with my grandmother – and for the first time I realised that maybe she wasn't as boring as Andy Murray.

You know that feeling when you're prepared for something? Like you feel proper good if you're prepared for an exam before you take it, or when you go to *Starbucks,* you know exactly what you want because you've placed that order so many times before. I don't think being a mum is anything like that... I mean is it gonna ask me questions which I don't know the answer to? Will I notice every single thing about it while it notices so little of me? Or will it abandon me once I've fallen madly in love with it? I don't know. Coz I'm pretty sure we ain't actually built for more than one heartbreak?

3.2

Final Confession to Mum

She turns on her camera for the last time.

SHAHEEDA — I did it. I fell in love and I got pregnant, and I know you did the same, even if you never tell me. This year, there have actually been times when I've felt like I've died and gone straight to heaven, you should know that, and it's been right here in Hounslow. My dreams, and the stuff that goes through my head is mad, so mad that if you saw it, you would probably put me in some kind of institution. I swear down, I have been listening to what Uncle Abdul Azeez says about us girls! How we're extra precious and that we have more duties and all that but my dreams are too big to think like that – and I don't care what Uncle says, Mum! We're definitely supposed to be free... just as free as everyone else. Before I go I want you to know...

(We hear the sound of the alarm go off which she set earlier on in the play, she gets startled and begins to panic. She then paces up and down her room knowing she's out of time, she finishes it off.) That I get it... and I'm sorry.

(She signs off and moves towards the camera to shut it down, she goes over to her alarm and turns it off, emotionally

charged by the fact that she's run out of time. She then places the last few items in her suitcase and zips it up. She makes her bed and then puts her duffel bag on top of her suitcase and pulls up the wheeling handle ready to leave. She takes one final look at her room. She then stops and turns to the audience.)

Hounslow Girl. I know what you're thinking; I know what you're thinking! 'Hounslow Girl'... A lost little Hounslow Girl with no real prospects or grip on reality and I can see it written all over your faces! *(Pause)* I might have known what I was gonna do all along but I ain't lied about anything, maybe I told you too much but I couldn't just tell you the basics or you'll just chalk me up as another Tracey Brooker which I know you wanna do, coz it will be easier and we all know that there's a better chance that I'm guaranteed happiness out there. I'm guaranteed first-hand wisdom and I can actually be taught something without someone having to teach me, coz I've come to realise that you don't really learn anything real from people, and I still have all these questions that no one here has the answer to! And I ain't got time to answer them myself because that's what I've been doing here this whole time, answering my own questions! And that's all I've got coming my way. Questions! Questions from everyone! About this year, about the

future about life! And I ain't lived mine
so don't ask me yet! I don't care if Allah
ever forgives me for doing this either!
(She looks up towards the ceiling) Coz
I can feel you breathing down my neck
right about now. I don't care if you ever
forgive me! Because you're the one who
put me in this mess! It's your entire fault.
I mean what is this obsession you have
with giving people happiness and then
snatching it away? I don't need someone
else to tell me about the Seven Wonders
of the World and how I'm gonna feel
when I'm stood in front of them. I mean
who actually decided on the Seven
Wonders of the World in the first place?
Some philosopher of some kind decided
that Niagara Falls is more beautiful than
the marble caverns in Chile, or the Great
Wall of China is more breathtaking than
the Shara Bridge in Yemen! From the
Great Pyramid of Geeza to the Northern
Lights! Whatever! They were built by
people! They were built by people,
people who can recognise beauty! People
who felt like they needed something
exquisite so it could distract them from
the boring places that you created in
the first place! I mean I used to speak
to Uncle about the Seven Wonders of
the World and he was convinced that
Mecca was one of them, innit? I used to
have to tell him, 'Bruv', it's really *not*,
but to him it was. To See, To Hear, To
Touch, To Taste, To Feel, To Love and

to live... could they be the true Seven Wonders of the World? I'll stay, I'll face her, face this and give it all a go. *(Pause)* I know growing up starts with taking some kind of responsibility and seeking forgiveness from those you've hurt. From the people who are here... from her. Her who looked after us and tried her best to protect us, her who carries paradise beneath her feet like Uncle Abdul Azeez says that all mothers do and I don't think I could have ever really seen it through her eyes until now... when I realise paradise will soon be beneath mine. *(She puts her suitcase to one side and pushes the wheelie handle down. She then moves the chair to the middle of the room and places the chair for her mum to sit on. She looks at it and then sits on the floor next to the leg of the chair.)* The feelings I have now won't disappear overnight, but somehow, someway.... everything will be alright. *(She smiles to herself.)* I ain't dumb. I'm intelligent enough to know, that I don't know anything. And do you know what? I think that might get me through.

Blackout.

The End.